Sail the Seven Seas
of Freedom

Sail the Seven Seas of Freedom

Living the Pirate Lifestyle

Captain Rob Lee

Bella Rose
Global Publishing

Sail the Seven Seas of Freedom, Living the Pirate Lifestyle

ISBN-13 978-0-9826542-0-0

Bella Rose Global Publishing
P.O. Box 1418
Sarasota, Florida 34230
publisher@svBellaRose.com

10 9 8 7 6 5 4 3 2

Logbook Contents

Foreword

The Good Life Parable
(Story of the Mexican Fisherman)

The American businessman was at the pier of a small coastal Mexican village when a small boat with just one fisherman docked. Inside the small boat were several large yellow fin tuna. The American complimented the Mexican on the quality of his fish and asked how long it took to catch them.

The Mexican replied only a little while. The American then asked why didn't he stay out longer and catch more fish? The Mexican said he had enough to support his family's immediate needs. The American then asked, "But what do you do with the rest of your time?" The Mexican fisherman said, "I sleep late, fish a little, play with my children, take siesta with my wife, Maria, stroll into the village each evening where I sip wine and play guitar with my amigos, I have a full and busy life, senior."

The American scoffed, "I am a Harvard MBA and could help you. You should spend more time fishing and with the proceeds, buy a bigger boat with the proceeds from the bigger boat you could buy several boats, eventually you would have a fleet of fishing boats. Instead of selling your catch to a middleman you would sell directly to the processor, eventually opening your own cannery. You would control the product, processing and distribution. You would need to leave this small coastal fishing village and move to Mexico City, then LA and eventually NYC where you will run your expanding enterprise."

The Mexican fisherman asked, "But senior, how long will this all take?"

To which the American replied, "15-20 years."

"But what then, senior?"

The American laughed and said that's the best part. "When the time is right you would announce an IPO and sell your company stock to the public and become very rich, you would make millions."

"Millions, senior? Then what?"

The American said, "Then you would retire. Move to a small coastal fishing village where you would sleep late, fish a little, play with your kids, take siesta with your wife, stroll to the village in the evenings where you could sip wine and play your guitar with your amigos."

Reprinted with permission from the author and my friend -
Dr. Mark Albion, More Than Money

Preface

"Normal is getting dressed in clothes that you buy for work and driving through traffic in a car that you are still paying for - in order to get to the job you need to pay for the clothes and the car, and the house you leave vacant all day so you can afford to live in it." Ellen Goodman

When I started writing this book my original "working" title was **Your Life Sucks - My Life Doesn't Suck, Why**. It went through several revisions and changes with the assistance and input from friends. I finally selected the title **Sail the Seven Seas of Freedom**.

Why did I start out with this working title? Why does your life suck? Maybe it started when you attended the college your parents wanted you to attend instead of the college you wanted to attend. Maybe you moved into a charming house in a proper subdivision with an appropriate car in the garage, when you really wanted a comfortable log cabin on a beautiful lake with a dirt covered 4-wheel drive pickup truck in the driveway, or any other multitude of reasons. The point being, most likely you are living the life expected of you rather than living the life you expected.

This book is about how to live a not normal life in a normal world. I am not going to tell you if you give up your lattes and cigars, work really hard, and live well below your means during the best years of your life you can be happy and have fun when you are old. The work ethic rules of the normal world are culturally created illusions. Rules are made up by people to control other people and pirates do not follow rules. I want you to be doing what you want to be doing and not what the rules say you should be doing.

Sail the Seven Seas of Freedom is about changing the way you view the world and your life. The purpose of this book is showing you how to enjoy life each and every day. I will help you rediscover your core values and give you the strength to listen to your inner voice. I want you to stop living an unfulfilling deferred lifestyle and start living a happy, fun, exciting, and fulfilling lifestyle, one with complete freedom! My goal is to help you live the life of your dreams NOW by sharing how we left a normal life and began living the life of our dreams.

This book will show you how to live a Mexican fisherman's life in the American businessman's world.

Captain Rob
SV Bella Rose
Somewhere on the water
September 2009

Prologue

The captain's logbook is a form of record keeping that has been around since humankind began sailing the seven seas. Within the logbook are kept the details of the ship's course, the rate at which she sails, the weather, the wind, such matters as turn up every day, or hour, and with a short account of every event which occurs during a voyage.

Sail the Seven Seas of Freedom is Captain Rob's logbook and contains within the details of his voyage to living the pirate lifestyle.

Captain Rob's Log - Freedom

Herein ye shall find th' riches t' sail t' freedom if ye will sail th' seas wit' Captain Rob

Captain Rob's Log - Introduction

About Captain Rob and why you should listen to me.

First and foremost I live on a sailboat, full time. Yes, I am a terrific example of sailing the seven seas of freedom and living the real liveaboard pirate lifestyle. You can say, *"I'm not just talking the talk, I'm walking the walk."*

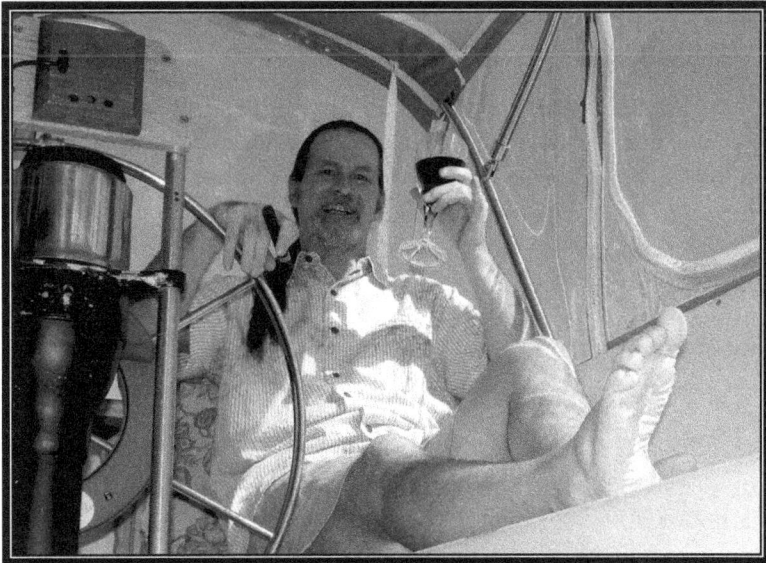

It's 5 o'clock somewhere!

I have spent my life learning and perfecting the secrets of how to live the Pirate Lifestyle, studying what works and what doesn't work. Most of it I learned the hard way because there wasn't anyone available to teach or show me what to do. Yes, I have had a lot of fun learning, however, it sure would have been more fun to have an expert to coach me.

"There are only two ways to live your life. One is as though nothing is a miracle. The other is as though everything is a miracle." Albert Einstein

Life is about doing. Life is about action. Life is about having FUN! If what you are doing is not making you happy, it is time to do something different. One day I had a revelation and asked myself, *"What the heck am I doing?"* I don't recall the exact moment that this happened, but it did. I had my **"Aha"** moment. It could have been almost anything that caused my awakening. I had gotten comfortable. I was living my life in neutral, treading water and going nowhere. Time for a change! From that fateful moment I was consumed with the need to do something "different" with my life, to create and live my own reality.

When I told my family I was going to move on a sailboat I got that "deer in the headlights" blank stare. I know everyone thought I had gone crazy. Humor him, play along, and he will come back to his senses. Oh well, I have always marched to the beat of a different drummer.

Time t' march t' me owns drummer me hearty.

So we stumbled through the steps of moving aboard a sailboat. No single, unique right way exists, to leave land and move aboard a sailboat. I will let you in on a big secret (don't tell everyone) there is no wrong way to do it. Trust me. Obviously we figured it out. It wasn't easy. Sure, we faced many challenges doing it on our own. We continued onward, learning, doing, and having fun.

Now all the naysayers are asking me how I did it. Many that once thought me crazy are now envious of my liveaboard pirate lifestyle. I can only smile when they say, *"You are so lucky to live on a boat I wish I could do it!"* The truth is they could do it too if they really wanted to and I am going to share my secrets with you.

I have written several works that have been published in newspapers, magazines, and on the Internet. For example, "Our Unexpected Adventure" in *Living Aboard Magazine.*

I have done it. I am doing it. I am having a BLAST! I know what I am talking about, and I can help you do it too. Why? Why am I willing to share my experience and knowledge with you? Because helping you sail the seven seas of freedom, helping you create and design your personal pirate lifestyle (no you don't have to live on a boat) is my way of helping make the world a better place.

Like watching a caterpillar transform into a butterfly, helping you make your dreams become reality, makes me feel good. Giving is super fun and knowing I have helped you improve your life is my reward.

Arrr! Let's kick the tires and light the fires.

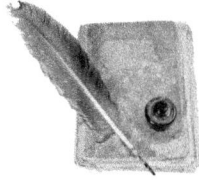

Captain Rob's Log - Why

Why live the pirate lifestyle?

Before we go any further, I want to say something. I want this to be an informational logbook, but I also want it to be FUN so read it with a laid back cheerful attitude.

You have made the decision to sail the seven seas of freedom and live the pirate lifestyle. Now what? It appears overwhelming. Trust me, you are not alone. Living the pirate lifestyle in today's noisy world is no easy task. But then you already know that and that is why you are reading this. So let's get on with it shall we…

Yo ho, yo ho, 'tis th' pirates life fer me.

For me, the "why" live the pirate lifestyle seems it should be a given. I mean why wouldn't you want to live the pirate lifestyle? Just in case "why" is not apparent to you, here is why.

Sailing the seven seas of freedom and living the pirate lifestyle is an awesome way to live life. It is a delightfully romantic and peaceful way to live. Nothing beats waking up on the water, sipping coffee in the cockpit, and taking in a big breath of fresh clean air. The freedom of going wherever you want whenever you want. Yes, freedom. In the complex modern world a freedom few will ever experience. Why, because they have an unfounded fear of change. Think about it. People fear leaving the security and comfort of their home. All the while, their house is attached to a rock hurling through space.

Reality is negotiable, you have a choice. Today is the perfect time to reexamine your world, your reality, and make changes so you will take advantage of the many opportunities that exist. You see the world though your eyes, and you create your universe and your reality, by the experiences you live. Your reality has been created by people around you, parents, teachers, bosses, friends, and the media are a few examples.

"Reality is merely an illusion, albeit a very persistent one."
Albert Einstein

How do you change your reality? Here in lies the problem, you cannot create your new reality thinking and seeing the same way that you have been thinking and seeing. You cannot solve a problem with the same thinking you used to create the problem. If you want to do something different with your life, you must do something you have never done before. Start focusing on your dreams and stop being a normal world victim.

Everything begins with making a decision. So start making decisions that rewrite your reality and thereby rewrite your life. Take charge of your life and head in a new direction that takes you to the reality of your dreams. The goal is to have fun and live a happy and rewarding life. Focus your mind and rewrite your reality. It is all just an illusion. It is all just a game.

Take charge o' yer universe 'n paint yer dream reality me bucko.

"Security is mostly a superstition. It does not exist in nature, nor do the children of men as a whole experience it. Avoiding danger is no safer in the long run than outright exposure. Life is either a daring adventure, or nothing." Helen Keller

Reality is an illusion and job security is an illusion too. A normal job, a job at a big company is not a secure job. Recent events have shown us all there is no guarantee of long-term income, health benefits, and pension working for a large corporation. Just because you are getting a paycheck doesn't make it a secure paycheck. To repeat, working hard and exchanging your time for money at some big company has no job security.

"But Captain Rob, I have bills to pay, I have a family to support, and working for myself is risky."

The vicious circle of clothes, house, car, commute, traffic, and work is the big trap of a normal life with a normal job. Security is an illusion unless you own the job, meaning you are your own boss. Time is your most valuable asset (as far as I can tell we just get one trip through life), so don't let some company boss tell you what your time is worth. Risk is not the opposite of security. Insecurity is the opposite of security and risk is the solution, the answer to you finding and creating security. Again, you must step outside your comfort zone and do something you have never done before.

When ye thirst t' discover new oceans ye must 'ave th' courage t' lose sight o' land. Arrr.

Sailing the seven seas of freedom and living the pirate lifestyle is unlike any normal lifestyle. In my opinion, it offers a higher quality of life and plenty of security. We are bombarded with so many things we have no control over. Most of us suffer from information overload. Television news goes round and round about mindless issues. What can you do about any of these issues? Why do we make life so darn complicated? Life really is simple and all you need to do is simplify your life. Complexity is something you must remove from your life. Focus on developing your pirate attitude. Start thinking and acting like a pirate. Become more passionate about your goal.

Living the pirate lifestyle really becomes a state of mind.

Too many people put on clothes they buy specifically for work, leaving a big house with a huge mortgage empty all day, driving in rush hour traffic with a car they are still paying for, in order to get to the job they desperately need so they can pay for the clothes, house, and car. Huh? Living the pirate lifestyle allows you to build a life that reflects your values. For me it is about being independent, self-reliant, self-sufficient, and in control of my life.

"As you simplify your life, the laws of the universe will be simpler; solitude will not be solitude, poverty will not be poverty, nor weakness weakness." Henry David Thoreau

The last reason to live the pirate lifestyle could be personal survival. I don't want to come across as a conspiracy theory doomsday fanatic, but... We are living in a world where any disaster of several kinds can disrupt life as we know it. Maybe it will be a natural disaster like another enormous hurricane, or a huge flood, or a giant earthquake. Maybe it will be something far worse. Are you prepared? Can you survive a disaster that paralyzes emergency resources? Most people in this country wouldn't be able to survive on their own. We survived a hurricane, living without a source of food and water for weeks. We had no electricity for eleven months.

Just to be clear and I hope state the obvious, you do NOT have to live on a boat to live the pirate lifestyle. A boat is a place and the pirate lifestyle is a state of mind, something you may possess anywhere you might be.

Aye! Th' pirate lifestyle be a state o' mind.

Maybe I should be asking, *"Why aren't you already sailing the seven seas of freedom and living the pirate lifestyle?"* Think about it. This tells you a lot about yourself. Stop here. Before you continue, write down in the space on the next page, the reasons you aren't already sailing the seven seas of freedom and living the pirate lifestyle. I am serious, this task is very important.

Captain Rob Lee

The reasons you are NOT already sailing the seven seas of freedom and living the pirate lifestyle.

OK, let's get to it.

Captain Rob's Log - Attitude

Developing a positive pirate attitude.

Attitude is the result of the current, the flow, of your thoughts, ideas, feelings, and beliefs. To sail the seven seas of freedom and live a successful pirate lifestyle you must create and maintain an outstanding attitude. You are constantly developing your attitude, both in the direction of your influence on other people, as well as the influence other people have on you.

Life be too short, if it ain't fun then I ain't doin' it! Arrr.

The way you think affects your attitude. Day in and day out, your internal dialogue influences the way you handle daily situations. The human mind is like a computer, and you control the thoughts input and actions output. You are what you think. So, do you see the glass as half empty or half full? Do you say mostly cloudy or partly sunny? Seriously, do you say something like, *"What will happen if I lose my job?"* Or do you say, *"What can I do to start my own business?"* It is all in the attitude. Remove the words **someday**, **hope**, and **try** from your vocabulary. Replace them with the words **today**, **will**, and **do**. Thoughts can be very powerful and when they are mixed with purpose, persistence, and passion you will be a winner.

"Try not. Do or do not, there is no try." Yoda

Face the day contemplating what can be done and not stewing about what cannot be done. Accept complete responsibility for your own thinking, your own attitude. Envision what you desire to accomplish. Visualize the end result in your mind. Define the goal you wish to achieve. Break this goal down into smaller, doable steps, and start doing it. Like a motorcycle rider on twisty road, look where you want to go to and go there. Do not focus on the obstacles in your way, like the ditch, or that is where you will end up. Look beyond the immediate obstacles and visualize successfully reaching your goal.

Most people go through life complaining about their lack of success. They see other people, "lucky" people, moving steadily forward to their goals and they feel if they possessed these same qualities they would attain the same desirable results. Sadly, and incorrectly, these people assume they can never possess these positive qualities. Wrong! The truth is, anyone can completely change their attitude. As already stated, the human mind is like a computer, and can be programmed with undesirable traits and characteristics creating a negative attitude, or desirable traits and characteristics creating a positive attitude.

Ye attract th' thin's ye be expectin', so be expectin' positive thin's.

With a positive attitude, one of confidence and fearlessness you will be less affected by negative, pessimistic thoughts. We all know people who radiate failure, discouragement, and "*I can't.*" And, at the same time, we all know people filled with confidence, courage, enthusiasm, and "*I can.*" As you encounter obstacles, you must react in a positive way. Other people will put your positive attitude to the test, but only you control your attitude unless you give that control to others. You decide whether you are happy or sad, joyful or angry, trusting or jealous, courageous or fearful, composed or anxious, and contented or envious.

Without question, your success is directly dependent on your attitude. We must regularly monitor and adjust our attitude. Most people rarely think about their attitude and they certainly don't think about changing it. Your attitude is totally in your control. On a happiness scale of ONE to TEN, with TEN being abundantly happy and ONE being ready to walk the plank, where do you see yourself? Ye better be sayin' TEN, matey!

Th' beatin's will continue 'til yer attitude improves.

"Attitude – The difference between an ordeal and an adventure." Bob Bitchin

Having fun is an important part of attitude management. Studies show wonderful benefits from laughter. Humor is also very important to cultivating a positive pirate attitude. The more fun you are having, the more you will accomplish. If you haven't noticed, there is frequent use of humorous pirate speak in this book. Having fun is a priority in the life of everyone who wants great happiness. You can convert life's stresses into fun with an attitude shift if you focus on maintaining a sense of humor in your daily life. With a lighthearted attitude, events that would normally be annoying will be laughable. Having a sense of humor is a critical part of having fun. Make your own fun instead of waiting for it to come to you.

Circumstances beyond your control constantly happen and will continue to happen. Everyone encounters hard times, everyone encounters obstacles, and the challenge is to stay on the road and out of the ditch. It is not what happens to us that matters, it is our attitude and how we respond that matters. Are you asking, *"How can I change and improve my attitude?"* You are constantly building, creating, and adjusting your attitude. Both in the direction of your effect on other people as well as the effect others have on you. Stop focusing on what you don't like and start focusing on what you do like. Then take action on your new positive thoughts.

Adjust yer attitude, me hearty. Ye will be havin' more fun.

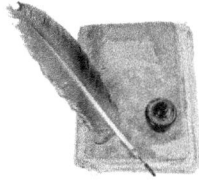

Captain Rob's Log - Focus

Focusing on what must be done.

I have been thinking about why some people are able to take action and some people never accomplish anything. You know what I mean. Some people talk about their dreams, all the ambitious goals they "plan" to carry out, but they never actually do anything. Or maybe they complain they cannot get anything done because there are not enough hours in the day. I am sure you can think of examples of people not realizing the goals they desire to achieve.

One answer is "Shiny Things" distractions.

Because we live on a sailboat, let me use this lifestyle as an example and hopeful solution. When you are cruising, life is simple. All you have to do is stay alive. That's it! Nothing else matters or is important. You eat when you are hungry and you sleep when you get tired. If something breaks, you fix it. For example, if you develop a leak in your boat you fix it RIGHT NOW. Not tomorrow or the next day. Everything you do serves a purpose and you don't question why. The world is black and white and there are no distractions, you simply do what you must do to stay alive.

Doin' wha' ye must do 'n how t' stay alive today.

Captain Rob Lee

In our modern civilized complicated world our lives are filled with meaningless decisions. If you are hungry do you eat at McDonald's or Burger King? No, maybe we should eat at Subway this time? Do I start a blog on Wordpress or Blogger? Should I mow the lawn today or tomorrow? Television!?!?! OMG don't get me going on this topic. Talk about a waste of time. Do I watch Fox, CNN, or MSNBC? I just googled this, as of November 2008 American households' watch eight hours and eighteen minutes of TV each day. Damn! That is one third of a day right there.

OK Captain Rob, calm down, let's move on...

So the world is in a financial crisis. Yes, a lot of people are getting hurt because they are living a normal life. Bad things like people losing their jobs and homes are happening all around us. Guess what? A lot of people are also living the life of their dreams because they are in control of their existence. Which person will you be?

Will Ye be Proactive?

Are you letting circumstances beyond your control dictate how you live life? It is easy to let outside influences drive us away from our goals. We convince ourselves that we are managing. After all, we are busy and things aren't really that bad. Are they? Most people don't like change and you need to become uncomfortable to accomplish your goal of living the pirate lifestyle. In fact, many people truly fear change. Most people will remain the same, until the pain of staying the same exceeds the pain of changing. No matter how hard you try, you cannot avoid pain. Remember, stuff happens in life. You and I cannot stop unplanned circumstances from happening. Sail your life to where you want to be.

> *"I can't change the direction of the wind, but I can adjust my sails to always reach my destination."* Jimmy Dean

Spend your time on the things you can change and don't waste your time or energy worrying about things out of your control. We cannot change world economics any more than we can change the direction of the wind. All we can do is adjust our lives to accept what is occurring all around us. We can always get to where we want to go, but we must be willing to change direction and take a different course to get there.

Are Ye Focusin' on Results?

To paraphrase Tony Robbins, *"Standing in your weedy garden, with your hands raised to the heavens, chanting 'no more weeds, no more weeds, no more weeds' isn't going to do a darn thing."* You must accept your garden is full of weeds, get down on your hands and knees, and start pulling.

Figure out where you are now in your life. Take responsibility for your current situation. Also, you must know where you want to go to and set a course to get there. Create a list of goals. Make a plan, figure it out, and do what it takes to get there. Remember, achievers focus on results and underachievers focus on obstacles. Know who you are and resist negative outside influences. You are what you see and hear. Spend your time seeing and hearing things that move you closer to your goals. Don't simply accept your life as it unfolds. Again, sail your life to where you want to be.

So how do we apply the *"doing what must be done"* cruising life to living a complicated modern world life? Few situations in our daily lives are truly life threatening. Simplify life by focusing on what is important. Evaluate each choice, if *"it's a hole in the boat"* then deal with it and if it is not, don't worry about it. Life is full of events that we must manage. When we are in the moment the situation might seem or appear impossible. Think back through life: high school, dating, jobs, cars, bills, marriage, children, and aging parents, whatever. We all have been in difficult, often impossible circumstances. Somehow we survive and we are stronger because of all we've been through. If it is not a hole in your boat don't worry about it! Accept that we cannot control and change everything. A sailboater cannot control the wind all you can do is adjust your course. If a big storm comes along you must deal with it, you cannot put it off until tomorrow. The important decisions are easy because they aren't decisions at all. Unimportant decisions waste our time and the outcome is of no consequence. Do NOT get distracted by all the mindless busyness of the complicated world and focus on what must be done.

"The average man will bristle if you say his father was dishonest, but he will brag a little if he discovers that his great-grandfather was a pirate."

So be a pirate! Make your great-grandkids proud. Do what must be done as if your life depends on you getting it done, because it does…

Captain Rob's Log - Timing

The time is never "right."

If living the pirate lifestyle is important to you, and I assume it is you have to jump in with both feet. If you are waiting until the time is right, it will never happen. All the roadblocks to sailing the seven seas of freedom and living the pirate lifestyle are in your mind, what you believe you can or cannot do.

"If you think you can do a thing or think you can't do a thing, you're right." Henry Ford

You must stop doing what other people around you are doing. Most families no longer work together toward a common goal. For example, how many people do you know that eat meals as a family? Be honest. In order to succeed in life and create your pirate lifestyle you must ignore conventional thinking. You must do the opposite of what other people are doing. When everyone else makes the easy choice and is paddling downstream, paddle upstream against the current and find your own way. Everyone will tell you, *"You are going the wrong way."* When you want to take control of your life you must start doing everything for yourself.

Do nah listen to th' naysayers, me bucko.

Life is full of choices and the only failure in life is *"no choice."* People who succeed reach decisions promptly. Life is about attitude. Life is about perseverance. Life is about having fun. Life is about doing, not dreaming. You cannot live life in neutral, when life is comfortable it is easy to keep doing nothing.

> *"In any moment of decision, the best thing you can do is the right thing, the next best thing is the wrong thing, and the worst thing you can do is nothing."* Theodore Roosevelt

Fear is a powerful emotion that prevents us from doing what we must do. Fear of failure, of losing everything will paralyze you. Don't let this happen! Fight fears with courage and fearlessness. Look at all the top achievers in the world: actors, athletes, musicians, and entrepreneurs. They each took the path of their passions. Many risked everything and were willing to endure extreme sacrifice to achieve their goals. Remember, if it is not a hole in your boat don't worry about it. Be willing to risk it all!

How far are ye willin' ta go? Are ye willin' to risk it all?

Every action you take is either moving you closer to or further from your goal of living the pirate lifestyle. Go to the store and buy a calendar. Get a big enough calendar to comfortably write on and hang it up on your refrigerator. Pick a date less than one year from today and put a big red X on that day. This date is the day you will be completely, without exception, sailing the seven seas of freedom and living the pirate lifestyle. If you pick a date too far in the future, it will allow you to procrastinate. You will start making excuses and it will never happen. So pick a date approximately one year from today and stick with it. Now you have made the commitment, you have put it in writing, and you are not allowed to change this date.

"I am an old man and have known a great many troubles, but most of them never happened." Mark Twain

Start now! Take action and start moving toward living the pirate lifestyle today. Not tomorrow, or next week, or next month. Remember, every choice you now make, must be moving you closer to living the pirate lifestyle. The only essential attributes that you need to start sailing the seven seas of freedom and living the pirate lifestyle is, ***"Wanting to do it bad enough."*** That's it!

"But, Rob, I have a job and a house and kids in school and elderly parents. I need more time."

No you don't.

I had a small business. I had a big house. I have kids in school. I have an elderly (sorry mom) parent. We did it. We did it and I am not gifted with any special talents.

The commitment was made and kept. Whether we were ready or not, we were going to live our pirate lifestyle on a sailboat. Yes, the last few weeks before we moved were crazy busy. But we never strayed from the goal to go. On August 1st, just two weeks past our scheduled departure goal, we pulled out the driveway, trailer loaded to the top with all our material belongings.

Let me share the story of packing our trailer. We looked into renting a truck to haul our things from our home to our sailboat. We were in Maine and our sailboat was in Louisiana, a long way away from us. The cost was ridiculous and the time issues of pickup, drop-off, and how long we could have it overly limiting. So we decided it would be better to purchase a trailer. In hindsight, it was a good decision. Anyway, I taped off a spot on the floor of our family room the size of the trailer. We used a yardstick for the height of the "trailer-space." Everything we intended to take with us had to fit in that space. The two of us had frequent heated debates about what to take and what to leave behind. Each of us had our own ideas about what was important and what wasn't important. We packed and repacked box after box of stuff. I cannot begin to guess the hours we spent determining what to take and what to leave behind. We actually shipped a few boxes of things to the marina that we *needed* but wouldn't fit on the trailer. Looking back on that time, we could have left behind half the things we brought with us. Our advice to you, most of what you think you need, you don't really need, and you probably won't ever use the stuff.

Sorry I wandered off-topic. I tend to do that. The subject of this logbook entry (chapter) is timing. The main points being, the timing is never right, you are never completely ready, and you must make decisions. You must make the commitment to start living the pirate lifestyle and stick to it. Every day there will be challenges to overcome. Some might seem or appear impossible. We could have easily gotten distracted in our trailer packing ordeal. It was difficult but we stayed focused on our goal to live the pirate lifestyle.

Th' time ta go be now matey.

Captain Rob's Log - Debt

The correct place to start is?

Ready? The correct place to start is your financial situation. Sorry! You want to sail the seven seas of freedom and live the pirate lifestyle then you must face the debt demon now. Freedom is the key to living the pirate lifestyle and you cannot be truly free obligated to others with debt. You hunger to live free and no one can be free buying stuff with credit. It is pretty simply really, if you cannot afford it, then YOU CANNOT AFFORD IT! Say, "NO" to debt and indebtedness.

'tis when pirates count thar booty that they become mere thieves.

Loads of books are available on the subject of finance and money management. Many financial experts are more than willing to tell you how you should live your life (for a small fee). Let's agree to the fact that there is no one right way to do this. I am sharing the steps we followed and sharing what worked for us. In 2004 I calculate my monthly expenses. At that time I needed to generate nearly $11,000 income each month to pay my bills. **Eleven Thousand Dollars!** My vehicles alone; a truck, two cars, a jeep, and a motorcycle, with their insurance were costing me $3,500 each month. Today, we pay slip rent when in a marina, we have limited insurance on our sailboat, and we have a cell phone bill, totaling approximately $600 each month. That's it! The long-term goal is freedom and this logbook entry explains the path we followed to successfully achieve our financial freedom.

I don't like talking or thinking about where money goes anymore then you do. American culture trains us to spend more money than we make. As I stated earlier, the biggest problem is in our heads. Shaped, molded, and trained to spend spend spend, buy buy buy. We are a nation based on, out of control consumption. This step requires massive action. In order to live free and enjoy the pirate lifestyle you must reduce you spending and become debt-free. No one can be free and indebted at the same time. Once your life is under your control and you are living the pirate lifestyle, you can relax. We did this and you can do it too.

This be about understandin' where ye spend yer doubloons.

It is time to take a long hard look where and how you spend your money. Write it all down every single bill, debt, and financial obligation you have. Yes, this might be a painful process but you must stop pouring money down into a hole in the ocean.

List ALL of your bills, debts, and financial obligations. Here is an example list to get you started.

Mortgage or Rent:

Car Payment:

Visa:

Mastercard:

Gas station card:

Department Store cards:

Add other cards:

Electricity:

Gas:

Phone:

Cell Phone:

Cable TV:

Internet:

Insurance:

Gasoline:

Food:

List all other bills:

Now list the ones you forgot:

Look at all your financial obligations and eliminate all you can. Those you cannot eliminate, reduce the payment as much as you can. For example, raise the deductible on your car insurance. Reduce the monthly cable bill by cutting back on the service. Better yet, have it disconnected. Maybe drop the land phone line. You could (should) stop eating out at restaurants. Consolidate your car trips. Don't drive ten miles for a late night pizza. Being even more aggressive, you might consider moving to a less expensive house/apartment. You should sell the car (or cars) if you have a monthly payment and pick up an inexpensive one for cash. Yes it is a sacrifice but you have a goal. If the expense is not moving you closer to your goal of living the pirate lifestyle, get rid of it. I think you get the picture.

"When you're in a hole, stop digging." Denis Healey

To be really hard core about this, all you need to be paying for is shelter and food. Ouch! No, we didn't go to this extreme. I am throwing ideas out there. You do need to examine and understand where the money is going. As painful as it was, I sat at the kitchen table and listed all our bills. The sooner you stop the bleeding, the sooner you can achieve your goal of living the pirate lifestyle. We would have never been able to move aboard a boat if we kept spending at the level we were then spending at. Trust me when I say we had a lot of debt (goes along with the $11,000 needed income). It was really hard work and it wasn't any fun. However, it was a wondrous relief to be free from the debt once it was gone. I can say without hesitation, I never want to go back to being in debt. NEVER!

Every rapscallion must be tempted, at times, t' spit on his hands, hoist th' black Jolly Roger, 'n begin slittin' throats.

To be crystal clear, I am NOT against spending money, or having an expensive home, or fancy cars, or other big-ticket belongings. When you can PAY for them! The point is to say, "NO" to debt and credit. This logbook entry is not about spending the money you have, it is about getting out of debt as quickly as possible. When you want the freedom the pirate lifestyle offers, heck when you just want to be free and happy wherever, you must get out of debt. The pirate lifestyle is about being happy and having fun. If you owe a bunch of money, you won't be able to focus on having fun and probably not be very happy either.

As I said in the first paragraph, say, "NO" to debt and indebtedness. I strongly suggest you completely stop using credit cards. Put aside cash for each expense, like groceries and gasoline. This way you won't waste money on a $3.00 cup of coffee when you fill up the car with gasoline. Yes it is a sacrifice but you have a goal. Nothing in this life is free. You must be willing to give up something in order to get something else. Stay focused on the goal of living the pirate lifestyle.

We do not have one single credit card, nada, none, not a one. We have not had a credit card for about five years now. Believe me when I say we had a bunch of them. So stop ye whinin' matey, I know ye can do this.

Aye me bucko. Th' pirate lifestyle be about bein' free, bein' debt free.

Captain Rob's Log - Income

Make more money.

    This logbook entry is about the other side of the money equation, creating ways of earning more money. The previous logbook entry was about slowing and stopping the outflow of money, and this logbook entry is about increasing the inflow of money.

    Disclaimer, this logbook entry is a temporary solution to the income side of the equation. Clearly, the following suggestions are short-term solutions only. The long-term goal is freedom and the long-term income solution is so important that it has its own logbook entry.

I reckon I feel a change in th' wind, says I.

    If you have a job, you might consider going to your boss and flat out asking for a raise. Just don't say why you want it! Maybe you can put in more hours at work, ask to work some overtime. However, in today's economy this might not work very well. If you have your own business, as I did, you could work more hours. For example, you can take on an additional client or customer (or two or three). Another option might be to get a second job? The first job is to pay the bills and the second job is to fill the booty chest. Yes, I know it stinks. Sorry. How bad do you want to live the pirate lifestyle?

Early in my adult life, after graduating from college, I had two jobs (actually I had three jobs). Job number one was a salesperson at a regional retailer and job number two was a bartender at a local bar. I walked to the retail job early in the morning. At 5 o'clock p.m. I was picked up from job number one and while being driven from job number one to job number two I changed my clothes in the backseat of the car. At 1 o'clock a.m. I walked home from the bartending job and went to bed. In my free time, I sold vacuum cleaners door to door. I knew this was not how I wanted to spend my life but I did this for about one year.

So suck it up and do what you have to do to make the move to living the pirate lifestyle. You have to be willing to do whatever it takes to get ahead. Just look around, and decide what you can do to make extra money.

Being self-employed, it was relatively simple for me to work additional hours. Not easy, but simple to make additional money. When we made the decision to move aboard I started working a little extra time every day. I squeezed every nickel I could out of my business, knowing it was only for a short time. All the extra money I earned went in the booty chest. No exceptions!

Now 'n then we had a hope that if we lived 'n were good, God would permit us t' be pirates.

Your ultimate goal is to increase your relative income. You must stop thinking like everyone in the normal world, *aye ye be a pirate now*, and their concern about absolute income. What do I mean? Here is an example. Person-1 is an executive with any big company and works 80 hours per week earning $200,000 a year. Person-2 is a pirate working part-time and operating a small business from their boat. Person-2 works 8 hours per week earning $20,000 a year. Which person earns more? Why? Are you starting to understand relative income? Crunching the numbers, both people earn an identical hourly wage. Person-2 has substantially more freedom. Remember money alone is not the answer. Having the time, the freedom, to do what you want when you want to do it is more important. You can always make more money but you cannot make more time. Relative income is a measure of money and time. It is all about the freedom.

"But Rob, I'm confused." I know, on one hand I am telling you to go out and make more money. To work, work, and work some more and all the while saying work is not everything that time is

worth more. While the overall topic of this logbook is totally against working hard now and deferring life until later, sometimes one must do something for a short time to get where you want to go. When we made the decision to sail the seven seas of freedom and live the pirate lifestyle, I worked hard, paid down our debt, and saved all I could for FOUR MONTHS. I am not talking about doing this for years and years. This is why I suggested in the logbook entry **Timing**, to buy a calendar and pick a date less than a year from today and why I stated a disclaimer at the beginning of this logbook entry. Remember, the need to work more right now is to remove all the debt you have acquired and to build up your booty chest. Call it the price of admission to a better life, the pirate life. Once you have the credit cards paid off, the car paid off, everything paid off, and some money in the booty chest then and only then will you be able to enjoy your time living the pirate lifestyle.

Th' happiest pirates are pirates wit' a full booty chest.

Captain Rob's Log – Letting Go

Start selling your stuff.

Too many people think having "nice" things will make them happy. Wrong. We all collect "stuff" for no good reason. Physical clutter leads to emotional clutter, mental clutter, and even spiritual clutter. We must let go of material clutter in our lives before we can rewrite our reality and begin living the pirate lifestyle.

Ye can nah loot it wit' ye anyway, so get rid o' it!

People keep things just in case, never throwing anything away, and hoarding junk for a rainy day. Do you have a closet full of clothing and you usually feel you have nothing to wear? Do you have boxes and boxes full of stuff? Do you remember what is in those boxes? From a young age we are taught that acquiring material belongings makes us successful and happy.

Clutter is a kind of obstacle, like big rocks interfering with the flow of water in a river. When your life is cluttered with "rocks" it requires great energy to move. Removing these rocks allows you to move along easily. If you are feeling overwhelmed, remove the clutter and make room for the way you really wish to live.

Declutter yer world 'n free up yer life t' do wha' ye really wants t' do.

Stuff does not make you secure and treasuring material belongings increases the energy needed to keep the stuff. It is a false sense of security and a false sense of self-worth. Physical clutter becomes a huge weight like an anchor. When you rid yourself of the physical clutter, you also remove all the mental distractions, the energy drain, freeing yourself to do what you really want to do. Instead of you owning material things they own you. For example, I did not own my vehicles the bank did and I paid for them, every month financially and emotionally. Even if you don't have a bank loan against something, it still owns you because it is a physical and mental burden. True happiness comes from freedom, family time, and positive self-esteem. You want to be free and live the pirate lifestyle.

Like everything in your life, look at the items and determine are they moving you closer to your goal, are they productive items? Or are they pulling you away from your goal, are they nonproductive items? Remember, we don't own material belongings, material belongings own us, and material belongings weight us down like anchors and chains.

Stop trying to justify the value of material "things."

Remember, it is all worthless stuff and treasuring material belongings you never use anyway, does not justify the money spent on the stuff. We had a garage sale to sell stuff, I bartered stuff, we gave stuff to our children, and we gave stuff to charity. What was left went to the dump. Today you have many more options to getting rid of stuff. The two online biggies, in my opinion, are Craigslist and EBay. Craigslist is a free service, you can list just about anything, but it is a local service. EBay is a fee service (costs money), they do have listing guidelines, and it has a wider audience. However, there is a bit of a learning curve and EBay is time-consuming to use.

When you start selling and giving away your material belongings the weight lifted off you is mind-blowing. Decluttering your world is freeing and freedom is what the pirate lifestyle is all about. Get over the foolishness of what you paid for it, what it is worth. It is not worth dirt. It is a great relief to let stuff go. You are investing in a new lifestyle. You must start thinking like a pirate. You absolutely must get over thinking and feeling material things have value. You aren't getting ripped off when you sell something for ten cents on the dollar. You got ripped off when you bought the crap. What is your new lifestyle worth?

Let go o' yer material thin's 'n make other scallywags happy.

"Letting go is really hard, but not as hard as holding on. You let go once. You have to hold on all day every day."

Material generosity is a great place to begin. For example, I sold my motorcycle to a family friend. He had always wanted a motorcycle but was too practical to buy one for himself. At the time he had two children in college. I made him a deal he couldn't refuse. The look on his face, the ear-to-ear grin, as he and his wife rode away on **their** new bike was well worth my "financial" loss.

To repeat myself, I am not against you, me, or anyone owning material things. My goal for you is freedom to live life, to live the pirate lifestyle. We were moving on a sailboat with limited living and storage space. If something did not serve an important purpose, it had to be eliminated. Your mileage will vary based on your life situation.

I can guarantee it will take much longer than you think to rid yourself of all the stuff you have collected. I can also guarantee you will wish you had started much sooner. Selling stuff is an emotional journey and it will be difficult. Use all the various options; family, friends, garage and yard sales, EBay and Craigslist, and local charities. These activities are time-consuming and drag out the emotional pain. If I had to do it over today, now knowing what is involved, I think I would contact a service where they come to your house, take everything, and hand you a check.

Getting rid of belongings you have collected over the years is liberating. You will feel your energy increase as you declutter your life. Learning to let go of stuff is an empowering experience. You will stop being a slave to materialism and gain your freedom. You will be able to live the pirate lifestyle.

How much freedom can you have?

Excellent question! Anyone, and I mean anyone, really can attain any level of freedom they desire. The best example that I can provide is to share our current degree of freedom. By now, you know we live on a sailboat. At any given moment, we are free to go anywhere we wish. All we need to do is untie the dock lines or weigh (raise) anchor and go. Bye-bye, we are gone. Seriously, right now I can take the helm and head for Mexico, The Keys, Bahamas, or anywhere we choose to go. Pretty cool…

"Wherever we want to go, we'll go. That's what a ship is, you know. It's not just a keel and a hull and a deck and sails, that's what a ship needs but what a ship is... what the Black Pearl really is... is freedom." Captain Jack Sparrow

Captain Rob's Log – Winning Mates

Associate with successful people, winners.

You are changing your reality and creating a new lifestyle. To strengthen your newly created reality, you must associate with, and build relationships with new people who have your new goals. Seek open minded, caring, and encouraging people to help you reach your goals and to become your personal network of positive thinking friends. Look for people who possess the qualities you would like to have. Also, find a mentor, a person or persons who will guide you along your journey.

Start talking with people living the life you dream of living. You want to sail the seven seas of freedom and live the pirate lifestyle, therefore, you must build and grow new relationships. Surround yourself with like-minded thinkers. Positive, successful people will energize you and motivate you. These successful, positive thinking people will share their wisdom and experience with you.

"Keep away from people who try to belittle your ambitions. Small people always do that, but the really great make you feel that you, too, can become great." Mark Twain

If you are like most Americans, you are comfortably living life in neutral. You have taken the normal path. You went to school then got a regular job with a steady paycheck. Last year you were

Captain Rob Lee

living paycheck to paycheck. This year you are living paycheck to paycheck. Unfortunately, next year you are probably going to be living paycheck to paycheck. Why does one stay on a sinking ship? I know why.

"Birds of a feather flock together." Proverb

Something known as **The Law of Association**, also known as mental association, states you will be like people you associate with, or, you become like people around you. In other words, you will be exactly like your closest friends. If your friends are losers you will be a loser, if your friends are winners you will be a winner too.

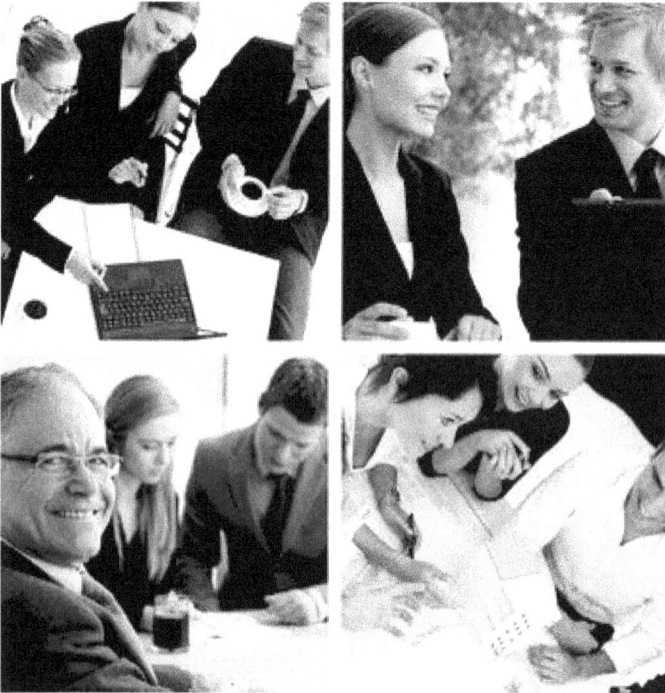

Me bucko, do ye wish t' stay th' same or change?

The only way to break this cycle is to get away from it. You must associate with people living how you want to live and not associating with people you don't want to live like anymore. You must get away from the negative influences in your life. *"But Rob, I can't just forget my friends."* Why not? If they don't support you, and they probably don't, they will attempt to undermine your plans. We all outgrow people. You are creating a new reality, you are no longer the same person, and people from your old reality can no longer relate to you.

What do you do with your current friends? Do you complain about things like work? Do you get together and whine about how unfair life is? Friends, coworkers, and family will try to talk you out of living your dream. They will say things like, *"How can you quit your job?"* Or maybe say, *"How will you pay the bills?"* Or even say, *"Why don't you put your dream on hold, until…"* It might not be so obvious but they will attempt to stall your plans. None of us knows how much time we have. Do not let others brainwash you into believing the timing will be better sometime in the future.

Associate wit' positive energy, like-minded scallywags. Arrr.

Without question, you need to associate with people who will encourage you. You need to hang around with, and listen to people who will help you reach your goal. I know this isn't easy, but friends come and go throughout our lives. Do you have the same friends you had in grade school? Do you have the same friends you had in high school or from your first job? If it were a choice between my current friends and my current life, or living the life of my goals and my dreams, I would choose my life, my goals, and my dreams.

It is all in your attitude, as discussed in the logbook entry **Attitude**. Don't see the glass as half empty, don't think of the relationships you will be losing, see the glass as half full, and think of the new relationships you will be gaining. If you don't let go of the old relationships, you will remain stuck in your old reality. It is important to focus on growth and developing your new reality.

For us, it was an easy transition and we jumped in with both feet. The fact we made the decision to move 1,500 miles away probably helped. We were so focused on creating our new reality that we didn't feel we were leaving friends behind. We kept our plans to move aboard a boat to ourselves. Not telling anyone, even our family, until the last month.

Find a mentor, consider yer goals 'n find someone ye admire 'n respect.

A mentor could be anyone you look up to and should be someone who possesses the qualities that you would like to have. It is important to have a good mentor, someone who makes you want to be a better person, someone who influences you in a positive way. There is nothing wrong with having a *"hero,"* someone you look up to as a mentor.

A mentor should be someone who has not forgotten where they came from. An expert might be wonderful to have as a mentor, however, a better mentor is often someone just a few steps ahead of you. A person able to assist you because they have come from the very same place you are now at. Also, do not limit yourself to a single mentor. You are growing in many different areas of your life as you create your new reality, so you should develop a relationship with many mentors. For example, maybe find a spiritual mentor or any other area you thirst to grow in.

Look at yourself and think about what you need and want. Your mentor will provide encouragement and help you assess your strengths and weaknesses. Ideally, your mentor will motivate you to be an active participant, to be a risk-taker. Look to people who inspire you and work at developing a relationship with them. Before you know it, you have a mentor!

Yer mentor will help ye sail th' seven seas o' freedom.

Captain Rob's Log – Long Term Income

Start a passive income Internet business.

A passive business is the long-term solution to funding your pirate lifestyle. This logbook entry is about building a passive income Internet business. In creating your new reality, this section is about unlearning the 9-5 work mentality and forgetting about the old-school concept of exchanging time for money. In the normal world, everyone works eight hours a day five days a week. WHY? Here you will learn how to design and develop a business that will operate on autopilot and will generate money day in and day out so you can sail the seven seas of freedom and live the pirate lifestyle.

Creatin' a passive flow o' doubloons t' fill th' booty chest.

All successful methods of making money on the Internet are versions of three basic systems: selling your own product or service, selling other's products or services (example: drop shipping), and affiliate programs (example: advertising). Internet marketing is not a get-rich-quick scheme. You will have to work hard, but making a steady monthly income is very doable. You don't have to be a Web site-designer. You don't have to understand HTML or other computer languages. You don't have to spend much money to start or bug your family members and friends to buy stuff. Anybody can do it. You can be smart or not so smart, educated or not so educated, young or not so young; whoever you might be, you can do this. The most important bit of encouragement I can give you is to get started and just do it.

One at a time, let's examine each of the three methods for making money and generating Internet income.

Affiliate Marketing

First, let's look at affiliate marketing. Affiliate marketing is where you list or link to other company's goods or services on your Web site. Depending on the company, you receive money when people either click an advertisement or purchase items. Two examples of the thousands of companies are Amazon and Google AdSense. Many companies now have an affiliate program. Without question, affiliate marketing is the easiest way to get started making money. You can be up and running in minutes. No kidding.

Aye! Doubloons t' fill th' booty chest in jus' minutes.

Once the system is set up, affiliate marketing is passive on your end. People visit your Web site, click hyperlinks you provide to merchants, and the merchants deposit money in your bank account. We are all familiar with the Google advertisements on Web sites we visit. We do not use Google AdSense on our Web sites, but many people generate an income this way. It is a simple process to signup with Google AdSense. Click their signup button and answer the questions. They "crawl" your Web site and pick advertisements that compliment your content.

Google AdSense

Earn money from relevant ads on your website
Google AdSense matches ads to your site's content and audience, and depending on the type of ad, you can earn money from clicks or impressions.

In my opinion, the average person is not going to make much money with advertising. Not unless you can get about a 100,000 or more visitors per month. The other thing I don't understand, just my opinion, why clutter up your Web site and waste limited space with someone else's advertisements? I want people to stay on my Web site and read my copy. I don't want them clicking off to some other Web site to spend their time and their money.

We do have a preference for affiliate programs like Amazon uses. Look at www.svBellaRose.com/recommendedreading.htm or at www.PirateLifestyle.com/recommendedreading.htm, these are our Amazon affiliate Web site pages where we recommend books to our members. If our visitors click the hyperlinks and purchase a product, we receive a small commission. We are not currently getting rich with this program, but it does generate income. Also, the service benefits our members and builds a stronger relationship with our members.

amazon associates

| Home | Links & Banners | Widgets | aStore | Reports | Developer Tools |

Earnings Report Totals   Glossary

July 1, 2008 to September 30, 2008

	Items Shipped	Revenue	Referral Fees
Total Amazon.com Items Shipped	26	$382.04	$19.23
Total Third Party Items Shipped	17	$175.84	$9.56
Total Items Shipped	**43**	**$557.88**	**$28.79**
Total Items Returned	**-1**	**-$22.44**	**-$0.90**
Total Refunds	**0**	**$0.00**	**$0.00**
TOTAL REFERRAL FEES	42	$535.44	$27.89

Selling other's goods or services

Next, let's discuss selling other's products (example: drop shipping method). At this time we do not do drop shipping, so I cannot offer first-hand knowledge of this method. It is a popular system and appears to be easy to get started in, very similar to the affiliate program we discussed earlier. You set up an e-store Web site and market physical products. Pick anything you might be interested in. Your e-store is open twenty-four hours a day and seven days a week. When someone purchases a product from your Web site you collect the money (full retail), then the drop shipper mails the item to the customer, and you pay the vendor the wholesale price. As an example, we purchased a new CD/DVD for our laptop computer on EBay. The seller is a drop shipper selling thousands of items each month. The challenges I see with drop shipping lie in finding a reputable company, finding quality products, and dealing with high overhead. If the opportunity presents itself, I would consider adding drop shipping to our Internet business.

Another method of selling other people's products is the joint venture arrangement. Joint ventures are a very popular method of building an Internet income. You form an agreement with another Internet business and recommend their product on your Web site. You can think of this as a more personal relationship than an affiliate arrangement. Typically you get a significant portion of the sale, unlike drop shipping. Many Internet small businesses are more than willing to share the revenues of their product for the increased visibility. Most joint ventures are between established Internet businesses that already have a friendly relationship.

In my opinion, selling someone else's products is the second-best way to make money on the Internet. If you are genuine with your copy and knowledgeable about what you are selling, you can make money this way.

Selling your own goods or services

Finally, let's explore the method of selling your own products or services. This concept should be familiar to everyone. It is not unlike any hobby-turned-home business. You create a product and sell it. Maybe you make jewelry or some other handcrafted item. People like to buy homemade products. Home based craft (hobby) turned business offers many opportunities.

We started a loose leaf tea Web site www.teasemeteas.com (no longer selling loose leaf teas). Here we sold our own label loose leaf teas. Obviously we didn't actually make the teas ourselves. We focused on just a few products. We both enjoy drinking tea. Tea has been a part of my life as long as I can remember. At the time, a tea Web site seemed like a good idea. It wasn't. We discovered there was way too much competition, and to be honest we didn't want to put in the time and energy trying to compete in an already crowded field. The lesson we learned, even if you are knowledgeable about a product you might be unable to make a profit selling the product. You need to be unique to make it in the Internet marketing world. A homemade unique handcrafted item could be a good Internet product.

Make sure that, if you decide to sell a product, you choose something you enjoy, understand, and can sell for a profit. Selling merchandise might be difficult for someone trying to be mobile, like us. We are on a sailboat and storage space is minimal. If you have the space and a good product, this might be a good option.

We recently opened a CafePress store. The basic CafePress store is free to own and operate. Here, we sell our own products, but the business operates like a drop shipping company. We started with a few items like hats, shirts, and a coffee mug and we will be expanding our online store because this service helps build a stronger relationship with our members.

cafe
press

Currency: USD ▼

sv Bella Rose Online Store

Categories:

Shirts (short)

Hats & Caps

Mugs

Hats & Caps

MORE COLORS AVAILABLE

Captain's & Admiral's Plain Cap
$16.49

Captain's & Admiral's Black Cap
$16.99

Ahoy. This be th' map t' th' secret booty.

The other half of this method is selling a digital service or digital information product. Digital information is arguably the best way to make significant money on the Internet. Why? You create an information service or product at little or no cost (mostly your time). You can then sell this service or product over and over and over. Look at www.svBellaRose.com/7secretstomovingaboard.htm on our Bella Rose Web site. Here we sell an information product that helps people make the move to living aboard. By sharing what we discovered while making the move aboard, we are motivating and helping others make the move to this wonderful liveaboard lifestyle. Look at www.PirateLifestyle.com/gooffgridgogreen.htm on our Pirate Lifestyle Web site. I started studying and using alternative energy in the 1970s. This digital product shares what I have learned and know about alternative solar and wind electricity.

~~89.00~~, ~~49.00~~ Pre-release Sale

Only 17.00

Buy Now

VISA BANK

Start Saving Money Today

This is a digital download. As soon as you complete your payment, you will be able to immediately start saving money with

- Going Green, Off-Grid Alternative Solar and Wind Electricity -

No waiting for your purchase to be shipped. How cool is that?

Once you have established your Internet business, you can sell your products using the joint venture arrangement. This time you are forming an agreement with another Internet person to sell your products on their Web site. Now this means you are sharing your profits with your joint venture partner.

Look at the many advantages to this kind of digital Internet business: no employees, low costs, no location requirements, automation, and you get paid over and over for your digital product. Selling your products with an online business is no different from running an offline business. You expand your business while building a relationship with your customers.

In my opinion, and it is only MY opinion, the only way to make any real money is to sell your own products. The best method to make this mobile and passive, so you don't have to be constantly online answering e-mails and driving to the local Post Office mailing packages, is to sell digital products. Creating and selling digital products is exactly what we are doing.

The key for long lasting success is what is known as the rinse-and-repeat methodology. As you figure out what works for you, you expand your income by adding additional products and services. If something is not working, move on and try something else, and when you find something that works rinse-and-repeat. Do it again and again and again, increasing your passive income.

Captain Rob's Log - Conclusion

Review and final thoughts.

We are living on a sailboat and enjoying life today and every day. I might get sick tomorrow, I might drop-dead tomorrow, and we might lose all our money or our sailboat. Both of us have parents that are getting older and they may require our assistance someday. If, and when any of this happens, we will deal with it. I refuse to look in the mirror each morning and say, *"Man I hate my life, but ten years from now life will be great."* There will always be something, some decision to be made.

> *"It is the set of the sails, not the direction of the wind that determines which way we will go."* Jim Rohn

The old-school idea of working hard, day in and day out year after year, at a job you don't really like, exchanging time for money, and deferring life until old age is going the way of the dinosaur. I strongly suggest you reread the **Foreword**, "Story of the Mexican Fisherman." Your goal is to live life each and every day, to have the freedom to do what you want to do when you want to do it.

Develop your plan of action and keep a journal of your journey. Start now and do this because you want to sail the seven seas of freedom and live the pirate lifestyle. The time will never be right. Start by reducing spending, eliminating all debt, and stop spending on anything that is not moving you closer to your goal of living the pirate lifestyle. Make more money anyway you can. If something does not serve an important purpose, eliminate it. Associate with people you want to live like and maintain a positive attitude. Start your passive income Internet business.

People who pursue thar passion are th' happiest people.

The greatest challenge in life it to find the thing you love. Please do not waste time living someone else's life. Listen to your inner voice and follow your heart.

Stay disciplined and focus on what you will be gaining and how much better your life will be. Like a motorcycle rider, look where you want to go to and go there. If you focus on the wrong place, like the ditch, that is where you will go so look beyond the immediate obstacles and visualize successfully reaching your goal. Push yourself to move forward, do something, anything, and keep the momentum going.

Read all you can. What books have you read in the past three months to improve the quality of your life? The secret to success is reading, learning, having a dream, taking risks, and taking action. Educate and prepare yourself for the ever present opportunities all around you. Study what other people have done successfully to live life to the fullest.

You have to do all this every single day. You cannot miss a day. Yes, it is hard work. You must act and make your own success by investing in your own well-being. Go now and don't be afraid to experiment. Remember what differentiates the winners from the losers: passion, persistence, and action.

Deferring life until later is like saving sex for old age.

You will make some friends along the journey, and you will leave a legacy to be forever remembered. Living your life today is the best way to live. We all create our reality and our own destiny. So go out there, make your own success and have fun doing it.

Go back and look at what you wrote down after reading the logbook entry **Why**. I didn't discuss it at the time on purpose. Do you see it not as a list of reasons but as a list of excuses? If you are not careful, the list of excuses will grow and grow until the list gets so long, you give up.

"For whatever the mind can conceive and believe, the mind can achieve." Napoleon Hill

Set your goals and focus on the dream to sail the seven seas of freedom and live the pirate lifestyle. Deeply feel the happiness and joy this lifestyle will bring you. Visualize the life you desire, take one day at a time, and remember it is all about having fun. Live each day like there is no tomorrow.

Please never take life too seriously, because it's all just a game, it's all just an illusion, and no one gets out alive anyway.

Ahoy! Wha' are ye waitin' fer me hearty? Arr.

If you have any questions, please ask. We are more than willing to help you because we truly want you to succeed. Please use the information in this logbook to create your own reality. I pray I have stimulated and motivated you to pursue your pirate lifestyle dreams…

"If today were the last day of my life, would I want to do what I am about to do today?" Steve Jobs

Sailing the Seven Seas of Freedom and Living the Pirate Lifestyle,

Captain Rob

rob@piratelifestyle.com

www.PirateLifestyle.com

www.ingramcontent.com/pod-product-compliance
Lightning Source LLC
Chambersburg PA
CBHW032033090426
42741CB00006B/802